MW01295538

OFFICE SPORTZ!

The OFFICIAL Office Games Handbook

BY
JEFF ROGERS
with
MARIA CORELL
KATE PORTERFIELD, PH.D..

Illustrations By
John Busser

iUniverse, Inc.
New York Bloomington

Disclaimer:

Office Sportz and the activities included in this book are for informational purposes only. Neither the authors nor the publisher is engaged in offering professional advice to the individual reader and/or company. The ideas, procedures, exercises, and suggestions contained in this book are for entertainment purposes only. None of the individual contributors, developers, sponsors, authors, or publishers of Office Sportz nor anyone else connected to Office Sportz can or will take any responsibility for the results or consequences of any attempt to use or adopt any of the information presented in this book.

Physical activity is not without its risks and this or any other program may result in injury. To reduce the risk of injury in your case, consult your doctor before beginning this program. The instructions presented are in no way intended as a substitute for medical consultation, the respective directors, officers, employees, publishers, authors and agents disclaims any liability from and in connection with these activities. As with any physical activity, if at any point during the activity you begin to feel faint, dizzy, or have physical discomfort, you should stop immediately and consult a physician.

User agrees to defend, indemnify, and hold harmless, Office Sportz, its contributors, any entity jointly created by them, their respective affiliates and their respective directors, officers, employees, publishers, authors and agents from and against all claims and expenses, including attorneys' fees, arising out of the participation or observation of any of the material and/or activities written or described herein.

Office Sportz
The Official Office Games Handbook

Copyright © 2008 by Jeff Rogers

iUniverse books may be ordered through booksellers or by contacting:

iUniverse
1663 Liberty Drive
Bloomington, IN 47403
www.iuniverse.com
1-800-Authors (1-800-288-4677)

ISBN: 978-0-595-53259-9 (pbk)
ISBN: 978-0-595-63314-2 (ebk)

Printed in the United States of America

This book is dedicated to everyone who holds down a job or multiple jobs, keeps their head low, and mouth shut in order to make a better place for themselves and their families.

We feel your pain.

You are the real heroes.

(Okay not really heroes, that was a little strong, but you get where we're coming from.)

CONTENTS

FORWARD

One of the most valuable lessons I learned was in ten below weather wearing a tight rubber suit and pointed booties. The sport was luge, the one where you lay flat on your back and scream helllllllllp all the way down an icy track of twists and turns. It was the national luge championships and fear had stopped blood flow to my head. The lesson came from a seasoned luge coach. He'd seen this numerous times before.

Before my impending, four G force, 70 mph run he leaned over and said, "Vince, before you go I want you to think about this. What did the one cannibal say to the other cannibal?" I stared at him in disbelief until he answered his own question. "Does this clown taste funny to you?"

I busted out laughing and then the coach said, "Have fun. You'll do great if you just have fun."

This lesson applies to life and the business of life. Office Sportz is a great tool to engage employees in a fun way. I wish I'd had this as a tool for our ski team.

Let me back up.

My luge career ended when I quit. (Funny how that works.) I wasn't enjoying it and didn't want to pay the price. But during the opening ceremonies in Calgary I watched from the stands while my former luge buddies were marching in as Olympians. Never again would I have that sting of regret. At the age of 26, with only a recreational skiing background, I took up the sport of speed skiing. In four short years I climbed to 10th in the world and a spot on the Canadian Olympic team. The single most important concept I used in this Olympian effort was a simple decision: Have fun!

Fun translates into peak performance. Think about athletes you see on television. Time and again, it is the athlete having fun who does well. Fun also affects teams as well. This is true in all levels of sport and business. Look no further than my nine-year old daughter when her basketball team went to the finals.

The other team of girls were playing and laughing. My daughter's team was nervous, rigid and uptight. Guess who won?

The team that made fun a priority!

Office Sportz is a wake up call for industrial revolutionary dinosaurs that reminisce through their pipe smoke about the good old days of command and control. After consulting and speaking to a hundreds of fortune 500 companies I have observed one inalienable truth. Companies that embrace the power of joy in the workplace make more money.

I trust this book will be a tool for you to establish a greater bond and sense of loyalty at work. It is through teamwork and employee engagement built into the modern office environment that will help us all succeed (even those funny tasting clowns).

Vince Poscente

Author of the New York Times Bestseller: The Age of Speed

PREFACE

*Warning: The following Preface is kinda serious; yet very important. The rest of the book is pretty entertaining, so we thought we should let you know ahead of time. Don't worry. It's short.

For the better part of 20 years, I have spent my life in service of corporations big and small, helping them to communicate their messages to their employees. As a Strategic Communications Creative Director and Professional Meeting Host I have seen every type of corporate culture you can imagine. But there is one striking similarity between all of them that drove me to write this book. Every person at every level of interaction, from CEO's to new salespeople, were all looking for one thing - ENGAGEMENT! Everyone wants the team to be engaged in their work but few people have figured out how to accomplish that task.

Until now.

Engagement comes from the combination of investing one's passion and energies plus the trust that those energies will not be in vain. Employees do not become engaged with a logo or a brand. They become engaged through the other people they work with on a daily basis. In World War II, Allied soldiers were asked what they were fighting for. Was it their flag, their country, their belief in right and wrong? Almost to a one they replied that while all of those things mattered, the most important thing they were fighting for was the guys in their unit or in their foxhole. They didn't want to let them down.

Now, corporate life rarely has life and death consequences, however the lesson can still be learned from our greatest generation: Engagement comes from being invested with those in your unit or division or sales group or HR staff. The people who go to work each day, spend eight or ten or twelve hours together in their foxholes and then come back the next day for more.

I believe it is a company's responsibility to create an environment that invites employees to invest in their co-workers and become engaged. It's better for the employees as they can share their passion for what they do with clients, vendors, VAD's, VAR's, neighbors, and anyone else who will listen. And it's better for the company because studies show that companies with more engaged employees have significantly better profits year over year.

Office Sportz was created as an easy way to start building or increase employee engagement. Office Sportz succeeds where other devices fail because it's an economical method of fostering teamwork while also nurturing outside the box thinking. All for the cost of some office supplies!

You can either do Office Sportz or pay for everyone in your office to go to Disney World with their families at the company's expense! Your choice. (Unless someone from Disney World is reading this book in which case you would all have to go to Aspen for a week.)

I hope you enjoy the book but most of all I hope this book acts as a fun way for you to offer your co-workers a place that is worth coming into every morning.

Good Luck and Let The Games Begin!

Jeff Rogers

INTRODUCTION

This book of exercises and games is guaranteed* to result in laughs, laughs, and more laughs. However, a fantastic thing can happen when a team works together on something enjoyable and, yes, even goofy: actual change can occur. By that, we mean that these games can be used to create an opportunity for real growth within your organization. No, none of your staff will come out of these games better at using PowerPoint or suddenly certified to do taxes. But, what is possible-if you use these games well-is that you can create an experience for your team that results in greater cohesiveness, improved trust and more healthy communication. Studies have shown that all of these results have the effect of raising employee engagement levels which is directly linked to a healthier bottom line.** And you'll have fun doing it! How crazy is that?

To those about to compete, we salute you!

The Authors-

Jeff Rogers
Maria Corell
Kate Porterfield, Ph.D.

*Guarantee of laughter not legally binding. No, seriously, its not.

**Yes, we looked it up: "Linking Organizational Characteristics to Employee Attitudes and Behavior," Forum for People Performance Management and Measurement

CHAPTER 1
GETTING STARTED

Use this book as a guide-a roadmap to creating 45 minutes, a half-day or a whole day of great activities for your group. There are no limits to what you can do. But here are some pointers for how to use this book:

There are several kinds of games in this book. Think about your group-what do you have on your hands? A bunch of eggheads who love a geeky analytical task? Jocks and athletes who are psyched for a physical challenge? A mix of all kinds of people-various ages, physical types and personalities? The latter is probably what you're dealing with unless you happen to have a strangely homogenous group on your hands (and we assume you're not the coach of an NBA team or the captain of a Yachting crew). If your group is diverse, you'll need to use the games creatively so as not to make someone really want to call in sick next time you say, "Hey, we're doing more office games tomorrow at staff meeting!"

Check out the book. We've arranged the games into four types. Chapter 2, Opening Ceremonies, is full of what we call "Warm-ups To Get Geeked Up With (also known by the fabulously fluid acronym: WUTGGU-don't try to steal that, it's trademarked.) They are great for any kind of group, but they are best used for a brief period, where they will mostly just get people laughing and feeling relaxed. There are many uses for these kinds of exercises, but they are especially good as punctuation marks on a meeting or other group activity. Use them to start off a meeting or after you've brought people back from a break. Use them at the end of a day to send people home in a good mood. Basically, these are just fun. But, watch what happens when people use them. You'll like what they do for your group.

Chapter 4, Individual Games, contains a collection of games that are fantastically fun and great for a group that feels comfortable moving around a bit if space allows it. Just give people some warning. You don't want to surprise people with physical tasks when they didn't see it coming. The lady in the 4-inch heels will be particularly annoyed when she's sprinting down the hall. Same for the guy in the three-piece suit.

Chapter 7, Team or Individual Sportz, contains games you can use to get the brainiacs in the group involved. They play to people's verbal and analytical skills and they are fantastic for making your group feel smart and clever. These games are great if your group is not the most physical crowd in town. They shouldn't land anyone in the Emergency Room unless someone strains their cerebellum.

Finally, Chapter 10, Team Sportz, comprises games that are the most dependent on teams working together. Basically, these games only succeed when people start relying on each other. Therein lies the really good stuff that can transform a group.

GETTING PEOPLE TALKING

We don't want to get too shrinky on you or anything (That's shrinky as in Head Shrink or Psychologist not "Wow that water is really cold, huh?"), but if you're going to put people through these games, you've got to know how to talk about the results with them. It's really important that you introduce the games in a positive way and then be ready to "debrief" them afterwards.

The intro is simple. We recommend something like, "Hey, guys, we're gonna try something different today. Let's have some fun and let's all try to participate. No nay-saying allowed."

The debrief can be your goldmine. That's when you get people to talk about what it felt like to work together, share ideas, be challenged in a new way, etc. The trick to debriefing well is to ask open-ended questions after the games. The simpler games will yield less (I mean how much can someone really say about shooting rubber-bands at celebrities' photos?), but don't be surprised if the higher-level, more complex games yield a lot of conversation. People may talk about their group process, their own personal styles of handling a challenge or just some realization they had about their job as a result of playing the game. Whatever they say, you want to make people feel validated and encouraged to speak more. (We don't recommend saying, "Wow, Bob, that was a really stupid observation," for example.) In order to help you with your debrief, we've included some questions that we think will get the conversation going. Don't be a robot and read them aloud - that will look really lame! Instead, just try to throw a few at the group casually after a game. If you just get blank stares, say "Ok, not much to say on that one, huh? Let's move onto another game. Try to notice how the next game feels and how our group behaves and then we'll talk about it afterwards, ok?"

Here are some basic debrief questions to use after a game:

* How did that game feel to you as a group?

* Did you notice anything about the way you felt during the game?

* How about the way our team functioned during the game?

* What did that game require?

* Were there any aspects of this challenge that reminded you of your job and what you have to do every day?

* What was the hardest thing about that exercise?

* Did anything surprise you about your own performance or anyone else's?

Add your own questions, of course, but be aware of how the tasks of the game may parallel tasks in your workplace - thinking on your feet, reacting to change, relying on certain team members, etc. And then get group members to realize the same thing!

PUTTING TOGETHER YOUR OFFICE SPORTZ EVENT

So decide what you want to do with your group. Are you looking for something quick and painless? Then, try STAPLER HUNT or PENCIL JAVELIN.

Want a longer, more challenging program? Then put together a half-day. It can look something like this:

OPENING CEREMONIES

WARM UPS

OFFICE OBSTACLE COURSE

PAPER CLIP RACE

SPELLING BEE

OFFICE AIRLINES

3-MAN BOBSLED

AWARD CEREMONIES

These are just two ways you could arrange things. The possibilities and combinations are endless! See what feels like a good fit for your group and try it out.

Just remember, the main goal is fun. In our opinion, that's what most offices really need. And that's what the "Office Sportz" are all about.

CHAPTER 2
OPENING CEREMONIES

Every great sporting event has an Opening Ceremony. The Olympics have the lighting of the flame; baseball and football have the singing of the National Anthem, and of course, let's not forget the brawl at the concession line for that last bratwurst. Here are a few suggestions to begin your Office Sportz games.

1. Each team must have an "office appropriate" name for their team which can be shown on posters, score tally sheets, and anywhere else they choose to display their propaganda.

2. Feel free to decorate the Opening Ceremonies area with crepe paper streamers, photos of the teams, signage, set the bosses desk on fire, etc. to add a festive look. Whatever works for your particular office is good with us.

3. Appoint a Master of Ceremonies who will stand on a box of computer paper and announce each team and its members to kick off the Opening Ceremonies. The MC will also show off the magnificent medals that will be awarded to the lucky winners. We recommend someone who absolutely does not want to play in any of the games. (It gives them something to do!)

4. Post a list of the events and the teams/individuals participating in them. Include time and place where each event occurs.

5. Begin with a Parade of Athletes dressed in their team regalia to appropriate music. We cannot recommend using John Williams' Olympic Fanfare which can be easily downloaded from any number of music sites, as that would entail unfair usage carrying a hefty fine.

Nope we do not recommend that music which perfectly fits this office event at all. (Our lawyers are all smiling now. It's not pretty.)

6. All athletes must recite the following pledge:

In the name of all office coworkers, I promise that I shall take part in these Office Sportz Games, respecting and abiding by the rules which govern them without doping and without drugs. I also solemnly swear not to brown nose with my immediate superior unless the opportunity is too good to pass up. I also promise not to hold my employer, Office Sportz, or any other entity liable for the inevitable pulled muscles, bruises, and/or unrelenting ribbing that may occur as a result of these games. I pledge to participate in the true spirit of Office Sportz-person-ship, for the glory of our workplace and the honor of (insert workgroup name here).

WARM UPS FOR ATHLETIC COMPETITION!

STRETCH

All good athletes must partake in some light stretching before competition. Have the group spread out in an open space to mentally and physically prepare for the athletic event of their lives. No one wants to pull a hammy in the "Office Chair High Jump."

DO THE WAVE!

Enjoy the camaraderie and spirit of Office Sportz by executing the communal deed that brings every group of sports enthusiasts together-the wave!

Form a circle with all participants. The Master of Ceremonies begins the wave and passes it around the circle. Continue this activity until the "whOOOOAAAA" sounds reach deafening levels or until it gets really annoying- whichever comes first.

THE FORBIDDEN STRETCH

Have contestants stand with their hands on their hips and their feet shoulder width apart. Start with the right hand. Have them raise it in the air as high as they are able, stretching the right side of the body. Then have them bring that hand back down, moving it across their body until it rests on their left hip, stretching their oblique muscles and their torso. Return it to rest on the right hip. Now, instruct them to move their right hands to their left shoulders, stretching their triceps, shoulder, and biceps. Repeat this same series of movements with the left hand. Raise it in the air. Bring it down across the torso to their right hip, back over to the left hip, up to the right shoulder and down. Repeat the entire process again, only this time do it faster and faster until everyone starts doing the Macarena. (Playing the music from the dance after a few repeats usually clues everyone in to the joke!)

WE ARE (INSERT COMPANY NAME HERE)

With the group still in a circle, the MC claps his or her hands together once and "passes" the clap to another player in the circle, making eye contact with them while saying the word "WE." The person to whom the energy was passes chooses another person in the group and passes that energy to them, clapping once, making eye contact and saying the word, "ARE." The third person receives the energy, chooses another person in the circle, makes eye contact and passes the energy to them with a clap and the name of your company. It's best in this scenario to use an abbreviated company name or initials for this portion of the game. If your company name is "Lutz and Arborgast Heating and Cooling" you may want to shorten it to "L and A" or another commonly used abbreviation known by employees. If not, this warm up could last longer than the competition itself.

When you conclude the three passes, begin the cycle again and try to make the rotation go as fast as possible, making "We are L and A" into a rousing team chant.

GO HANDS IN

To conclude the Opening Ceremonies, have everyone in the circle put a hand in the middle forming a stack of hands. When all are included, the MC yells, "WE ARE L and A!" All participants yell, "TEAM!", the circle breaks and the games begin!

CHAPTER 3
OFFICE SPORTZ
HISTORICAL TIMELINE

Here at Office Sportz headquarters, our crack research team of leading anthropologists, archeologists, sociologists, physiologists, meteorologists, paleontologists, ecotoxicologists, astrobiologists, gynecologists and unpaid interns have uncovered amazing discoveries that trace the history of Office Sportz back not only to the beginning of mankind, but the beginning of time and space.

TIMELINE- 5 BILLION B.C.- 151 B.C.

5 billion B.C.

Planet Earth forms. Meteors, asteroids and comets bombard newly formed Earth and compete to see who can make the biggest splash on the molten orb. Contest ends when Earth screams "uncle" and cools 1.5 billion years later.

3 billion B.C.

First signs of primeval life appear in oceans in the form of bacteria and blue-green algae. Bacteria devise contests to determine which could endure most toxic atmosphere and algae hold races to see which could photosynthesize first.

600 million B.C.

Earliest date to which fossils can be traced. Fossils of blue-green algae found most likely mid- photosynthesis race.

2.5 million B.C.

Homo habilis ("Skillful Man"). First brain expansion; is believed to have used stone tools to conduct the first recorded game of "Hammer Throw." The only differences? No tape, rock for paper ball and instead of hitting the basket most likely hit another Homo Habilis.

1.8 million B.C.

Homo erectus ("Upright Man"). Brain size twice that of Australopithecine species. Rumored to be excellent at grunting words in heated matches of "Spelling Bee."

1.7 million B.C.

Homo erectus leaves Africa in search of games that don't involve hand axes and antelope horns.

70,000 B.C.

Neanderthal man evolves. Ups the ante on first "DIY Obstacle Course" by lighting each obstacle on fire. Points deducted for singed body hair. Lowest recorded scores in "DIY Obstacle Course" history.

35,000 B.C.

Cro-Magnon man creates early game of "Unraveled" using strips of animal hide and a hollowed out turnip.

France 26,000 BC

Cave drawings found in the Cave of Cauvet depict half man-half ibex creatures throwing animal bones into a hole in the earth. One creature is being awarded a crude pendant made of flint and mammoth hair as what appears to be a defeated opponent gives him the finger.

10,000-4,000 B.C.

Development of settlements into cities and the development of skills such as the wheel, and pottery in Mesopotamia and elsewhere. Beginnings of the "Clay Pot Wheelie 500" races first recorded.

Sumeria 3200 BC

While mere mortals were developing stupid stuff like cuneiform writing, signs of impressive challenges occurred among the deities in the legendary "God of Air" vs. "Goddess of Chaos" games. When your office domain includes "watery bedlam" and "tempests and firmament," big time fun is sure to follow.

The Mother of Chaos, Tiamat, an immense dragon, announced that "3203 was her year to kick butt" and restore the earth to watery chaos. Upon doing so, she challenged "that Enlil, God of Air and Storms punk" to a smack down of epic proportions. Enil proclaimed "It's so totally on!" and an atmospheric game of "Bean Bag Bingo" ensued.

Using acres of sacrificed goat skins filled with grapes and flax, the highly contested, two lunar month battle concluded with Enlil the triumphant winner and fourteen days of unexplained darkness.

Enil's championship reign was short lived however when he was bested a century later by Ereshkigal, Goddess of Darkness, Gloom, and Death in an intense game of "Stylus Toss" (see "Pencil Javelin"). Ereshkigal emerged triumphant and the mighty God of Air and Storms met his fate - a colossal blast of dry heat resulting in instantaneous evaporation, crippling depression and eventual unemployment.

3000-2000 B.C.

Construction of the Great Pyramid at Giza (c. 2680 B.C.) and the Great Sphinx (c. 2540 B.C.) completed. First origins of "Hoop on a Loop" game employed during construction using not only a rope loop, but a rope loop and two ton blocks of stone. Contest took 23 years to complete and instead of yogurt lids with paperclips, winners were rewarded with ensured afterlife and the prosperity of all of Egypt. Whatever.

3000-1500 B.C.

Stonehenge erected in Britain according to some unknown astronomical rationale. Early pictographs etched into the dolerite stones represent builders celebrating the summer solstice by playing "Money for Nothing," tossing oxen bones against the Altar Stone and rewarding the winner with a "free cremation upon death" certificate.

Italy 800 BC

Just another boring day in Tuscany. Etruscans feel the "need for speed" and race newly introduced horse drawn chariots which replaced their old racing carts - olive crates rolled on the heads of Corsican slaves.

Greece 776 BC

According to legend, Greek god Hercules holds first games to honor his father, Zeus. First recorded game: "Shot Put Mouse" using a block of feta cheese and an actual mouse.

300-251 B.C.

First Roman gladiatorial games (264 B.C.). Challenges included "Sticky Note Fencing" with sharp swords and "Ringer Game" substituting Christians for rings and lions for cans.

250-201 B.C.

Great Wall of China built (c. 215 B.C.) as a result of an elaborate game of "The Amazing Big Block of Stone Race."

200-151 B.C.

Beginning of Roman world domination after victoriously defeating Carthaginians in an epic contest of "Wheeled Obstacle Course." In your face, Hannibal!

CHAPTER 4
INDIVIDUAL EVENTS

We were going to call it Singles Events but why should they have all the fun?

OFFICE STAPLES

Equipment: 10 staplers

Area: Large area with lots of cubes or merchandise.

Players: Limit 3 per round

Type: Individual

Time: 5 - 10 minutes max.

Objective: Locate as many staplers in the given area within a 20-second time frame OR find as many staplers in the best time.

Directions: Timekeeper hits the stopwatch. Contestants scramble for staplers in the given area. If done in cubicles, stapler hiding must be limited to non-intrusive areas, i.e. no drawers, purses, briefcases, under papers, etc.

Points: Points are awarded to those with the most staplers in 20-seconds or those with the most staplers in the shortest amount of time.

Safety:	No fighting, grappling or wrestling over staplers. Physical conflict today, even in the heat of competition, makes for awkward marketing meetings in the future.

SHOT PUT *MOUSE*

Equipment:	Computer mouse
Area:	Small carpeted area
Players:	6 - 9 max.
Type:	Individual
Time:	10 - 12 minutes max.
Objective:	Catch ball of mouse in hole as many times as possible in given time.
Directions:	Remove ball from computer mouse. With non-catching hand, toss ball straight up in the air and attempt to catch it in the computer mouse it came from.
Points:	1 point for every time the mouse ball is tossed into the air and caught in the mouse hole successfully.
Safety:	None

DIY OBSTACLE COURSE - OFFICE GAUNTLET

Equipment:	Computer, wheeled office chairs, boxes of paper, etc.
Area:	Defined by you
Players:	5 max.
Type:	Individual
Time:	Approx. 10 - 15 minutes

Objective: Complete the obstacle course in the shortest time possible

Directions: This is an event that your office can modify to fit the size and objects available in your given workspace. The challenges can be arranged in any order to fit the room. Example games are as follows:

Box Slalom Course:

        Line boxes of paper or file boxes in a row about 2 feet apart lengthwise down the alleyways between cubicles. Runner must begin at one end and zigzag left to right between each box to the end of the row. No walking, stepping or jumping over boxes.

Office Chair Strength Pull:

        Wrap a rope or extension cord around the middle of a desk chair a few times leaving equal lengths on either side approx 5' long. Fill chair with paper boxes, old computer monitors, books, etc., to make the chair heavy. Secure items in chair with duct tape. Contestants have to pull the chair as far as possible in the shortest time possible.

Speed Typing Test:

        Go to a designated computer in the obstacle course area. The computer should be set to a new Word document. Player must type "Now is the time for all good men to come to the aid of their country" or "Two all beef patties, special sauce, lettuce, cheese, pickles, onions on a sesame seed bun" 3 times with no errors. Player can correct as they go. Seconds will be deducted from the final time for spelling and punctuation errors left on the page after leaving the computer.

Points: Lowest time through the course wins.

Safety: Use your best judgment or ask someone with good judgment.

STICKY NOTE FENCING

Equipment: 3 in. x 3 in. sticky notes

Area: Circle 6 ft. in diameter

Players: 2 per round

Type: Individual

Time: Depends on number of players, 15 minutes max.

Objective: First person to pin 5 sticky notes on their opponent wins

Directions: Use sticky notes to mark a 6 ft circle on the playing surface. Judge gives contestants the go ahead. The first player to pin 5 sticky notes on their opponent wins. Notes are only to be stuck on arms, back and legs. Notes are not allowed to be removed during the fight and doing so will be grounds for disqualification. If contestant steps outside the sticky circle, one note is transferred from your opponent to you.

Safety: Be appropriate and respectful of your opponent during this challenge. It's not a race, so take your time and be mindful as you attempt to "stab" your opponent.

WHEELED OBSTACLE COURSE

Equipment: A wheeled desk chair, obstacles (see below)

Area: A large area is obviously needed to contain suitable obstacles - e.g. desks, photocopiers, and people, placed along the route.

Players: One at a time - 5 max.

Type: Individual

Time: 10 - 15 minutes max.

Objective: Complete the obstacle course while seated in the desk chair using mostly one's arms and limited foot use in the shortest time possible.

Directions: Timekeeper will give the go. It is recommended that each participant take a turn making their way around the course, using the obstacles to push themselves around and using only one foot for a pivot if necessary. "FOOT!" is yelled for unnecessary foot use and one second is added to the overall time for every infraction.

Safety: Make sure all obstacles are sturdy enough to push off of and secure any items that could be tipped over. Remove items from the top of heavy obstacles that could fall and cause injury.

PEN HUNT

Equipment: 2 identical pens

Area: Medium-sized common area with fair amount of merchandise or equipment.

Players: 3 - 5 max.

Type: Individual

Time: 1 minute each player

Objective: Find the pen hidden in the area in the least amount of time.

Directions: In private, the judge of the contest hides a pen in the playing area. Contestant #1 enters the area and is shown the pen that looks exactly like the one they are searching for. All other participants competing in this challenge must be out of the room. Judge/ Timekeeper gives the go and the contestant searches for pen #2. They have one minute to find the pen. Judge must decide before the game if they wish to add the "You're getting warmer/ You're ice cold" coaching hints. You can't decide halfway through the game as every player must have the same fair advantages.

When Contestant #1 is finished, the pen is hidden in the exact same place for the next contestant to find in order to provide an even playing field for all the athletes. Searching for a ball point pen is very athletic. Best time wins.

Safety: Hiding the pen under papers or partially out of site is permitted, however don't hide pen in an area that is too hard to find or a place that would be even mildly dangerous to reach.

PENCIL JAVELIN

Equipment: A few dull pencils, a tape measure, sticky notes to mark distances

Area: Long, open, people-free hallway or corridor

Players: 5 - 10 with 1 line judge to mark accurate distances and 1 judge at start line

Type: Individual

Time: 10 - 15 minutes

Objective: Throw pencil javelin-style as far as possible

Directions: Contestants stand at throw line and toss pencil horizontally, point-first down the corridor. The farthest toss wins.

OPTIONAL: Best grunt at release of javelin wins 1 extra inch to their best distance.

Safety: Make sure the pitch is clear of people at the time of throw. No "pimping out" javelins to increase weight or trajectory.

CHAMPIONSHIP OFFICE GOLF

Equipment: A paper coffee cup, golf ball, putter, scotch tape

Area: Preferably carpeted 10 ft. x 6 ft. space

Players: 5 - 7 max.

Type: Individual

Time: 10 - 15 minutes

Objective: 3 chances to putt ball into cup

Directions: Cut semi-circle from lip of coffee cup so it lies flat on carpet with nothing preventing ball from entering the cup. Putter gets three chances to hit the hole from 5 ft. away.

Safety: No chipping, no full swings, no conjuring Bob Hope's ghost. Caddyshack movie quotes are not only allowed, but encouraged.

RINGER GAME

Equipment: 3 or 4 coffee cans or empty gallon milk containers cut in half, 3 hoops made of sturdy cardboard - 2 ft. in diameter, tape for throw line

Area: 20 ft. x 20 ft.

Players: 3 - 6

Type: Individual

Time: 15 minutes

Objective: Set up the cans or containers about 5 ft. apart in the play area. Mark off a throw line about 10 ft. from the closest can

Directions: Each person throws the three rings at the targets.

A ringer counts as 1 point.

Put higher value on the cans as they get further away.

PHOTOGRAPHIC MEMORY

Equipment: Close-up photos of items or scenes around the work place.

Area: The entire office, immediate area, exterior and parking lot

Players: Up to 10

Type: Individual

Time: One day

Objective: Recognize as many things and places from the workplace where you spend at least 8 hours a day. Sounds easy, right? It's not.

Directions: Take about 20 photos of objects around the office location - the front door, a light post, the clock, the rug, a sign, a big rock. Some locations will be easier than others. Don't make objects or locations too obscure or go beyond the immediate office area. Make a list of each location photo with a corresponding number for judging later. Make blank lists for the contestants to fill out as the search for the locations.

Enlarge and color print the photos on computer paper. Assign the corresponding numbers from the judging list to the photos and hang them in a common area - 4 rows of 5 prints.

Each contestant has the day to identify where each photo was taken. At 4 p.m. the contestants must hand in their forms or be disqualified. The judge will then tally the score of correct answers and announce the winners.

Each correct answer is a point.

Patrol with the most points accumulated wins.

Safety: Players who find a location, object or setting cannot alter that location or setting to throw off other contestants. If caught doing so, they will be disqualified.

A TO Z IN 1-2-3

Equipment: Sheets of paper and pens for all contestants

Area: 10 ft. x10 ft.

Players: 5 - 7

Type: Individual

Time: 15 minutes

Objective: Alphabetically list as many objects in the category in the shortest amount of time.

Directions: Each person writes the letters A to Z on a sheet of paper. The judge calls out a category (e.g., food). The players have three minutes to create an alphabetical list of as many foods as they can think of; only one food is allowed for each letter of the alphabet. Contestants who write verified lists of 13 or more foods continue on to the second round of the competition.

Choose a different category for Round 2. (Category suggestions include things in nature, people's first names, famous people's last names, or cities.) At the end of three rounds, the person with the most verified appropriate items on their ABC lists is the gold medallist. The person with the second highest tally earns the silver etc.

TONGUE TWISTER TANGO

Equipment: Flip chart with one tongue twister printed on each page. An unbiased judge

Area:	Large open space
Players:	5 - 7 max.
Type:	Individual
Time:	TBD
Objective:	Exercise your elocution
Directions:	Use the Tongue Twister Database (Google it!) as your source of tongue twisters. Choose tongue twisters of appropriate length and readability for your players. Prepare flip chart paper so that a single tongue twister is written on ten different sheets. Arrange the tongue twister sheets from easiest to most difficult. Unveil the first (easiest) tongue twister. Provide time for contestants to practice saying the tongue twister fast three times. Then it's time for the competition to begin! One person who is not competing can serve as judge for the competition. The judge will arbitrate any disputes. The gold medal goes to the player who is able to say the most tongue twisters without being eliminated.
Safety:	Try to keep your language as office appropriate as possible.

CHAPTER 5
OFFICE SPORTZ HALL
OF FAME- DISCUS

SPIN CITY: WHIRLING DISCUS CHAMPION'S VICTORY HARD EARNED

Chad Boerman, systems analyst from Tacoma, WA, did not fully understand the importance of participating in the office Whirling Disc Us championship much less winning it.

Despite being born with a weak stomach, Boerman was coerced by his fellow IT team members into signing up for the Whirling Disc Us contest as part of the branch wide Office Sportz Challenge. Convinced his 20/20 vision and wrist agility would edge out the competition, Chad's coworkers employed an old-school, peer pressure full-court press.

"My motion sickness has plagued me since I was a kid." Chad explained. "I had a seizure once walking past a Tilt-a-Whirl. It's bad. So I told my team mates, 'Look, morons, I can hurl just watching a blender go round AND I had tuna salad for lunch. Nothing good can come from this!' But, of course, they wouldn't listen."

The team's persistence paid off and while Chad paid the temporary price for a jacked equilibrium, his high discus score helped IT tie Finance in final scoring. But the story doesn't end there. Ten minutes after the Whirling Disc Us competition but prior to the final score tabulation, Chad produced a technicolor yawn in the HR trashcan that warranted 10 extra points for vomiting, pushing his team to victory just minutes before the medals ceremony.

"I guess I'm a modern day hero," said Chad turning pasty white and wiping his mouth with his tie, "In the end, I'm just glad I could help out the team, ya know. I think I gotta sit down."

A modern day hero indeed.

CHAPTER 6
HISTORICAL TIMELINE

TIMELINE YEAR 1 A.D.-1900 A.D.

1-49

Birth of sand "3 Man Bobsledding!" Oh, and new calendars!

750-799

City of Machu Picchu flourishes in Peru. While building the "Lost City" Incan inhabitants create game "Perpetual Motion" as well as the lesser known and rarely used challenge "Small Pox Plinko."

c. 1000

Viking raider Leif Eriksson discovers North America and names it "Vinland." Possibly created earliest incarnation of "Office Airlines" by lobbing salmon from river to shore.

c. 1325

The beginning of the Renaissance in Italy. Early "Mouse Pad Toss" game created by flinging remarkably aerodynamic Botticelli paintings and measuring distance.

1453

Using small padded footstools to leap over, Turks conquer Constantinople in game of what we know today as "High Chair Jump" marking the end of the Byzantine Empire and the beginning of the Ottoman Empire.

1492

Christopher Columbus becomes first European to encounter Caribbean islands. While trying to communicate with islanders, creates first game of "Office Pictionary", and returns triumphantly to Spain with 10-15 kidnapped natives and a wicked strain of syphilis.

c. 1503

While devising an elaborate map for a game of "Photographic Memory," Leonardo DaVinci inadvertently creates blueprints for flying machine.

Renaissance England 1558-1603

The spark of competitive spirit flickered when a particularly agitated blacksmith from Kent hurled his firing tongs at a wandering minstrel sending him through the shop window. Soon afterward, the blacksmith and his apprentice began competing against one another, tossing tongs, anvils, hammers and various-sized pliers long distances in the town square for shillings bequeathed by wealthy passers by.

The contests were cut short, however, when blacksmith, apprentice and all wealthy passers-by succumbed to the bubonic plague.

1620

Pilgrims, after three-month voyage on the Mayflower, land at Plymouth Rock. While happy to no longer endure marathon bouts of "Pen Hunt," they are soon subjected to marathon bouts of typhoid.

1799

In Egypt, the Rosetta Stone is discovered containing text written in Egyptian and Coptic, then translated into Greek, demotic, and hieroglyphic script. While the text focuses on the great works of the Egyptian pharaoh, inscribed instructions for a primitive version of "Waste Paper B-Ball Smack-down" are included on the back.

1803

U.S. negotiates Louisiana Purchase from France. Documents indicate part of bargaining process includes game of "Great Balls of Paper" using wadded-up topographic maps of Arkansas.

1849

California gold rush begins. Think "Office Staples" but with gold, brothels and vigilantism. Go Niners!

1865

General Lee surrenders to Grant at Appomattox only after a final, best-outta-three game of "A to Z in 1-2-3."

1903

Wright Brothers, Orville and Wilbur fly first powered, controlled, heavier-than-air plane at Kitty Hawk, N.C. Played a quick, brotherly match of "Blindfold Putting" to determine who would man the craft.

1900s

Henry Ford and the Ford Motor Company develop first moving assembly line to produce the Model T. Early incarnations of wheeled "Three Man Bobsledding" by factory workers said to be the inspiration for the Tin Lizzy.

CHAPTER 7
TEAM OR INDIVIDUAL SPORTZ

The following games can be played by a team or an individual, thus the name of the chapter. Clever, huh?

CELEBRITY HIT CLUB

Equipment:	Medium to wide width rubber bands. Targets- 5 magazine photos of celebrities varying in size. One wheeled office chair. Copies of US Weekly, People, or In Touch magazine. Stopwatch
Area:	10' w x 6-7' d
Players:	Any #
Type:	Individual or team
Time:	Approx. 1-2 minutes
Objective:	Each famous face is ranked with highest point value for "overexposure" and/or "obnoxiousness" descending to "least annoying." The higher they rank on the scale, the smaller the photo and the higher the points awarded.
NOTE:	NO religious or political leaders. Only innocuous celebrities who would justify your using their photo

in this rinky-dink contest by chirping "any publicity is good publicity, right?"

Directions: While sitting in an office chair, participants have 10 seconds at each photo station to shoot as many rubber bands as possible at the target. When their 10 seconds are up, they roll a short distance to the next photo station. The athlete's goal is to accrue as many points as possible. The timekeeper tells the athlete when to begin shooting, when to stop, and when to move to the next target.

Feel out the group mind in regards to ranking your celebrities. Since it's unlikely you'll get a consensus on which celebrity is the most irritating, (one person's Paris is another person's Oprah) whoever is running the game must take this opportunity to make an executive decision and arrange the lineup as they see fit. Photos can be affixed to the back of lined up desk chairs or a wall.

Points: 1 point for least annoying celeb to 5 points for most annoying. "Most annoying" has smallest photo making it harder to score the big points.

Safety: Shooting other athletes constitutes disqualification and wallpapering offenders cube with left-over InTouch magazine photos.

RUBBER BAND ARCHERY #2

Equipment: Medium to wide width rubber bands. Stopwatch. A collection of desk toys, promotional junk or other objects offered up by willing donors. Some sort of ledge for lining up the toys. Preferably a large box, desk or cubicle on a hard surface to maximize destruction.

Area: Approx. 6-10' w x 6-7' d

Players: Any #

Type: Individual or Team

Time: Depends on # of players - 10 minutes max

Objective: Knock off as many toys in the row as possible in 30 seconds. The more damage you cause to the object, the higher the points.

Directions: Line the toys/objects on the ledge. Timekeeper tells athlete when to begin shooting and when to stop.

Make it clear to tchotchke donors that there is a strong likelihood their contributions to the Olympic cause will be disfigured, maimed or demolished. However, there is solace in knowing these toys will be relegated to the trash bin after sacrificing their inanimate lives in the name of semi-sanctioned corporate fun. This is more than they could say for themselves when they were sitting on your desk untouched, collecting dust.

Points: Olympic medals awarded for most toys/objects knocked off the shelf. Five extra points for mild-medium destruction. Ten extra points for obliteration.

Safety: See Rubber Band Archery #1 Safety and replace "In Touch magazine photos" with "leftover toys and promotional junk from this challenge."

WHIRLING DISC-US

Equipment: One desk chair, 5 compact discs, 5 wastepaper bins

Area: Semi circle with 7 foot radius

Players: Any number

Type: Individual or Team

Time: 10 minutes max

Objective: Get as many discs in the bin as possible...after being spun in a desk chair for 10 seconds.

Directions:	Athlete sits in desk chair, holds 5 discs and is spun 360° for 10 seconds. Immediately after stopping, the athlete must throw one disc at a time into the 5 bins places around the semi-circle.
Points:	Points are awarded for the most discs in bins. Extra points for vomiting. Automatic gold for vertigo.
Safety:	Spin with care.

HAMMER THROW

Equipment:	Scotch™ or duct tape, computer paper, one trash bin.
Area:	10 -12 ft.
Players:	Any number, 5-10 max
Type:	Team or Individual
Time:	Approx. 1 minute each contestant
Objective:	Throw paper ball using attached "tail" into trash bin.
Directions:	Take 4 pieces of computer paper and make a ball. Begin with one piece and add additional pieces around it. Use tape to keep it together. Make a 14-16 inch tail using yarn, string or Scotch™ tape. Attach tail securely to paper ball.
	Contestant stands 10 feet from empty bin and using the tail to throw, has three attempts to make a basket. Sound easy? Because the ball is relatively light and throwing with the tail gives you less control, scoring is actually a little harder than you think, Smarty Pants.
Points:	2 points per basket.
Safety:	None

Jeff Rogers; Maria Corell; Kate Porterfield, Ph. D.

MOUSE PAD TOSS

Equipment: 2 mouse pads

Area: An open area 10-12 ft long

Players: 5 max

Type: Team or Individual

Time: 15-20 min

Objective: Throw a mouse pad as far as you can while sitting in a swivel chair.

Directions: Participants must sit in a swivel chair at the start point and hold the mouse pads in their left or right hand. Standard mouse mats are mandatory for the event, no use of gel-padded mats allowed. On the shout of "hit it" the thrower must first swivel a full 360 degrees in the chair before hurling the mat as far as possible. The winner is the contestant who throws the mat the farthest without hitting a colleague.

Safety: Careful not to hit teammates. A mouse pad to the eye does not a fun Olympics make.

MONEY FOR NOTHING

Equipment: Two quarters, tape to mark the starting line, floor and wall target

Area: 10 ft from wall unobstructed

Players: 5 max

Type: Team or Individual

Time: 10 minutes max

Objective: Toss the quarters to hit the wall at the base or get closest to it.

Directions: Choose a bare wall in the office and place your start line approx. 10ft away from it. Participants take turns tossing quarters at the target. The winner is the one who hits the wall at the base or gets closest to it. For any tie-break situations, replay by moving one foot back each round until a winner is found.

Safety: Throw at target not opponent. Although this challenge is particularly strenuous, please resist the use of steroids.

OFFICE CHAIR RACING - THE WHEELIE 500

Equipment: Fully functioning wheeled desk chairs, tape for start and finish lines and a stopwatch.

Area: Long hallway with no stairs at either end

Players: 3 per heat

Type: Team or Individual

Time: 10-15 min max

Objective: Lowest time for race wins

Directions: Three racers, seated in their desk chairs, take their position at the starting line. Timekeeper yells go and starts the stopwatch. Each racer must stay in their own lane all the way to the finish line. Best time wins. Champion drinking a half-pint container of milk at medal ceremonies optional.

Safety: Weaving, crashing into other racers, leaving your lane, gluing plastic forks on your wheels to rip at your opponents ankles are all cause for disqualification.

HIGH (CHAIR) JUMP

Equipment: Two wheeled, armless desk chairs that can be raised and lowered to the same heights.

Area: Approx. 10 feet

Players: 5-10 max

Type: Team or Individual

Time: 10 minutes

Objective: Jump over chairs at highest point.

Directions: Space the two desk chairs seat-to-seat a few inches apart. Starting with chairs at their lowest height. jumpers leap over the seats. Jumpers are allowed a short running start to clear the chairs. If the chairs move from contact with the jumper's body at any point in the challenge, jumper is disqualified. When all have jumped their first round, raise desk chairs one inch and begin again, progressing to chairs' tallest height. If many jumpers still remain after highest chair setting, final tie breaking jumps will be awarded on style. Channel your inner Baryshnikov and make it happen!

Safety: Armless chairs are a MUST. Make sure chairs are spaced a bit apart so a crash landing splits the chairs apart from the middle.

THE AMAZING PAPER-CLIP RACE

Equipment: Boxes of paper clips (all same size)

Area: 10 ft. x 10 ft.

Players: 4 per round

Type: Team or Individual

Time: Approx 5-10 min

Objective:	Make the longest paper-clip chain in the shortest time
Directions:	Timekeeper starts match. Contestants hook paperclips together to form a long chain. Longest chain at one minute mark wins.
Safety:	Any evidence of doping in this event will result in disqualification.

BEAN BAG BINGO

Equipment:	5 beanbags, paper targets, tape. Bean bags can be made with dry beans and small size zip lock sandwich bags wrapped in duct tape.
Area:	15 x 15 approx.
Players:	Individuals compete for team points and medals.
Type:	Team and Individual
Time:	Rack up as many points as possible by tossing bean bags onto the targets.
Directions:	Tape the targets to the floor so they don't move. Define a throwing line ten or so feet away. Each person tosses the 5 beanbags at the targets. Those landing completely on the target gets 2 points, partial landings, 1 point.
Safety:	Throw bean bags at targets, not through windows. No eating the beans until the weekend...when you're alone... for a few days.

RHYTHMIC GYMNASTICS

Equipment:	Adding machine tape, paper, rulers- anything the gymnast wishes to make as their "flourish." Music CDs of any genre, CD player
Area:	15 ft. x15 ft.

Players: Up to 6 individuals, no more than 3 teams

Type: Team or Individual

Time: Each individual or team has 90 seconds to perform their routine. Individuals have 5 minutes to make their flourish and 5 minutes to rehearse their routine. Teams have 5 minutes to make their flourish and 10 minutes to rehearse their routine. (This can occur during the course of another event.) Actual competition running **Time:** 20-25 minutes.

Objective: Points(1-10) are awarded for creativity, style, agility, and dramatic interpretation. What you may lack in one area, you can make up in another.

Directions: Individuals: choose a song from the selection of CDs. Make your "flourish" and rehearse your routine. When it's your turn to perform, let your inner Nadia Comaneci shine.

Safety: Make sure your accoutrement is not likely to injure you or the spectators. You have a small space to work in so be mindful of your audience. And, while expressing yourself through movement, nothing inappropriate, sexual and/or disgusting, please. Perversion is grounds for job loss, possible lawsuits and most importantly, dishonorable discharge from the Office Sportz Event.

FLIP OUT

Equipment: A penny, a tennis ball or small rubber ball

Area: 10 ft. x 10 ft.

Players: Can be played in teams of two or player against player. Up to 5 teams of two or 10 individual players

Type: Team or Individual

Time: 60 seconds per round

Objective: Accumulate points with a teammate or individually

Directions: Place penny on the ground. Two players face each other, each about 4 feet from the penny. Players take turns throwing ball at the penny. Each hit on the penny is worth 1 point. Flipping the penny from heads to tails or tails to heads is worth 3 points.

Safety: This is no time to be practicing your overhand spike or attempting to bounce the ball so hard the rebound hits the ceiling. While fun and excruciatingly tempting, go easy with the ball...at least until everyone else leaves.

WHO'S ON THE ELEVATOR

Equipment: An elevator, poster, sticky notes

Area: A 10 ft. x 10ft. space around elevator entrance

Players: Up to 8

Type: Team or Individual

Time: TBD

Objective: Put your mental telepathy to good use.

Directions: At the start of the games, choose eight people to compete in the WOTE game. That morning each player attaches a sticky note to the poster with their guess as to who will exit the elevator closest to 2pm that day. At 2pm, a judge (preferably someone who sits close to the elevator and has full view of it) will monitor the elevator and see who gets off it as close to 2pm as possible. No two people can choose the same person.

Safety: No bum rushing the elevator passenger out of rage or glee. Clients especially tend to frown upon this behavior.

SPELLING BEE

Equipment: List of words from popular Spelling Bee contests.

Area: Large open space

Players: 5-7 max

Type: Team or Individual

Time: TBD

Objective: Spell for the gold.

Directions: Just like a regular Spelling Bee, contestants will be given a word and asked to spell it. They may ask for it to be used in a sentence, but that is all. We don't have all day.

The words will be of intermediate difficulty and get more difficult as players are eliminated. The last three standing receive medals with the final player winning the gold.

CHAPTER 8
OFFICE SPORTZ HALL
OF FAME- GOLF

CHAMPIONSHIP OFFICE GOLF IS A HOLE IN ONE FOR OHIO CPAS.

Sean Lackey, CPA from Westlake, Ohio said his company's office games sprang from sheer necessity.

"Tax time tensions run high in a CPA's office and anything can happen. You think because we're accountants we're mild-mannered people, but once I saw a female associate lift a Steelcase filing cabinet and toss it out a 5th story window. No one was hurt below because it was 3am on April 14th. She'd been there for 9 days straight and just lost it over some incomplete expense receipts. I couldn't fire her because a week earlier I nearly cut the jugular of a problem client with a letter opener. Hey, we all make mistakes."

Sean continued, "We needed some excitement in the office, so as part of an April 16th post-deadline day celebration, I suggested some office games to blow off some steam. It was Championship Office Golf that really made the difference. We cleared out a 6 ft. X 10 ft. square on the office floor, looked out over our fluorescent-lit vista of Berber beauty, lined up the coffee cup and our stress just disappeared!"

When all was said and done it was fellow CPA Randy Keyser that took #1 title. Randy explained "This 5 ft. course was no piece of cake golf course by any means. I mean look at the scores these individuals are shooting, 3 in a row, 2 in a row? That's a testament to the longevity and the perseverance of these guys and gals. They're tremendous players." How did it feel to wear the coveted green jacket? "It was really a green plastic table cloth left over from our St Patrick's Day party," said Randy, "but I felt like a champion in it. Just like Jack Nicholson! Wait. No... What's his?...Jack Nicklaus! Yeah! Jack Nicklaus."

CHAPTER 9
HISTORICAL TIMELINE

TIMELINE 1910 A.D.-2000 A.D. (ALSO KNOWN AS THE MODERN OFFICE SPORTZ.)

1910s

Albert Einstein publishes his Theory of General Relativity in 1915. After playing "Flip Out" with fellow patent clerks, Einstein began work on the development of general relativity which states that accelerated motion and being at rest in a gravitational field are physically identical. In short, if you were in a resting elevator and dropped the Flip Out ball to the ground it would have the same acceleration as a ball being dropped in an upward accelerating rocket ship far out into space. Yeah. He was wicked smart.

1920s

From the decade that brought you Prohibition, The Jazz Age, and the Scopes Monkey Trial, the airplane quickly became an integral part of American business during the 1920s. Air-Mail particularly became a quick success and as the public became increasingly infatuated with air travel, the game of "Office Airlines" swept the nation faster than you can say "Charles Lindbergh." Unlike today's email airplanes, 1920's paper planes were made from the pages of Orphan Annie comics and Sinclair Lewis novels.

1930s

The nation's love of Office Sportz is quelled when millions of people lose their jobs, savings, and homes during the Great Depression. Neighboring communities maintain their competitive spirit by holding races to see who can build the best Hooverville in 24 hours.

1940s

While most able-bodied men were fighting in Europe during WWII, in America "Rosie the Riveter" toiled on the home front making munitions and building airplanes. To blow off steam, the Rosies created the workplace sport: "How Many Gals Can Fit in the Wing of a B34 Bomber?"- a game that quickly disappeared post war.

1950s

IBM introduced new computers; NBC and CBS pioneered color television broadcasts and in 1957, the largest real-estate deal in U.S. history, a $66 million sale of William Zeckendorf's share of the Chrysler Building, occurred spawning a surge in popularity of the "Who's On the Elevator?" game.

Disneyland opens in California. In the spirit of magic, fun and imagination, park employees attempt to hold the first Office Sportz competition. The contests were cut short when large character heads lead to serious "Rhythmic Gymnastics" injuries and giant three fingered gloves make "Amazing Paperclip Race" impossible.

Ray Kroc opens his first franchised McDonald's restaurant in Des Plaines, Illinois on April 15, 1955. "Perpetual Motion" game is employed to help hamburger assembly line workers gain speed as the game "Is it Really Meat?" slowly loses popular standing.

1960s

The Beatles admit to playing games of "Whirling Discus" with Elvis LPs and a heated match of "Ad Exec" spawns the creation of the Black Panther Party. Neil Armstrong makes his descent to the Moon's surface and speeks his famous line "That's one small step for man, one giant leap for mankind" on July 20, 1969 Shortly thereafter the astronauts got in a few rounds of "Championship Office Golf" and a play a game of sans-gravity "Friday Night Flights" that took hours.

1970s

During the era that brought us the mood ring, public streaking and the Captain and Tennille on 8-track, President Richard M. Nixon is impeached as a result of campaign fraud, political espionage and sabotage, illegal break-ins, improper tax audits, massive-scale illegal wiretapping and a game of "Swivel Chair Curling" gone horribly awry.

Meanwhile, Stephen Hawking develops his theories of black holes based on a round of "Blind Fold Putting."

1980s

With heavy restructuring, celebrity CEO Lee Iacocca turns the ailing Chrysler Corporation around as his decisive and autocratic, albeit unorthodox, business methods produce quick results. In an effort to boost assembly line moral, Iacocca sanctioned intermittent rounds of "The Wheelie 500" using handcarts and industrial dollies. It is said that these makeshift vehicles inspired the K-Car line, including the Dodge Aries and Plymouth Reliant.

Using the wall as their target, a large mob of people playing "Rubber Band Archery" spark a public frenzy that results in the destruction of Berlin Wall in Germany.

1990s

Growing bored with group games of "Office Pictionary," Sony launches the first of the ubiquitous PlayStation series of console and hand-held game devices. Teen aged boys and man-children everywhere rejoice.

IBM launches its Thinkpad line of portable computers and the "Deep Blue" supercomputer defeats grandmaster Gary Kasparov in a six-game chess match as well as a round of Russian "Tongue Twister Tango." Deep Blue wins with "Cyvorotka iz prod Prostokvashi" as Kasparov weeps in defeat.

2000s

Reality television invades the airwaves. The initial idea behind popular TV program "Survivor" originated from producers observing CBS interns playing marathon games of "DIY Obstacle Course" and "Alpha Hunt."

Office Sportz publicly apologizes for its influence in this cultural television trend.

In this era of invasive tabloid journalism, games "Mystery Celebrity" and "Celebrity Hit Club" becomes smashing successes in Office Sportz contests around the globe.

CHAPTER 10
TEAM SPORTZ

The following games can be played by a team or an individual with multiple personalities. Like that guy from IT. You know who we're talking about.

TEAM SPORTZ

3 MAN BOBSLEDDING

Equipment:	3 wheeled office chairs. Masking tape for start and finish line. Stopwatch
Area:	Long clear area or hallway with no stairs at either end
Players:	3 per team
Type:	Team
Time:	Depends on the number of teams- 20 min max
Objective:	To be the bobsled team who travels the given distance in the least amount of time.
Directions:	Each bobsledder sits in their wheeled chair, one in front of the other holding onto the person's shoulders (NOT THE CHAIR) in front of them. The team begins completely behind the start line

and when given the signal begins their run. The timekeeper tells the team when to go and announces their finishing time at the end of the run.

Points: Awarded according to best time. Extra points if all members of your team are named "Bob."

Safety: It's important for the team to use their feet in unison to avoid bruised ankles and injured toes. Not recommended for team members wearing sandals. Make sure to hold the shoulders of the teammate in front of you and not the chair. Holding the chair could result in tipping.

SWIVEL CHAIR CURLING

Equipment: Rolling desk chair, 2 brooms, paperclips or washers, tape to mark distances traveled.

Area: Long hallway with smooth, non-carpeted surface. 10 - 15 feet clear rolling space and 10 feet sweeping space.

Players: 4 per team

Type: Team

Time: Approx. 10 min

Objective: Curler gives one push to a teammate who rolls down the "curling rink" while fellow teammates sweep paperclips or washers out of the way with broom.

Directions: Elect team positions- curler (pusher), curling stone (person in chair), and 2 sweepers. The curler gives one strong push to the "curling stone" that then travels a short, clear distance before approaching the paper clipped area of the lane. About 2-3 feet ahead of the approaching curling stone, sweepers begin furiously removing paperclips from the lane with brooms to ensure a longer distance for the stone to travel. Longest unobstructed distance traveled wins.

Points:	Points awarded for best distance (a la shuffleboard).
Safety:	Give unmanned chair a test run before each trial to check wheels. Obstruction in the wheels could lead to an abrupt stop and throw the rider.
	Use caution when pushing the curling stone e.g. if Todd from Accounting sits in the rolling desk chair, he cannot use his feet for acceleration, but "Curling Stone Todd" must be prepared to use feet as brakes ala Fred Flintstone.

WASTE PAPER B-BALL SMACKDOWN

Equipment:	Ball made from 5 pieces of computer paper, duct tape, trash bin
Area:	Circle with 7 ft. radius from trash bin and no walls for assists.
Players:	5-7 max
Type:	Team
Time:	Approx 10 minutes total or 1 minute each player
Objective:	Hit as many baskets possible in 5 attempts.
Directions:	Players sit in chair about 5 or 6 feet from trash bin and get 5 chances to score. You chair is likely to have wheels, so no traveling.
Safety:	A two-point score by the defense occurs when one of its players tackles an opponent in possession of the ball in his own end zone. Hold up...that's football. Never mind.

FRIDAY NIGHT FLIGHTS

| **Equipment:** | Nerf football or equivalent |
| **Area:** | 15 ft. x 15ft. |

Players:	2 per team - 4-5 teams
Type:	Team
Time:	10 minutes
Objective:	Keep the football in the air the longest.
Directions:	Each team must keep the ball in the air - no drops- for as long as possible. If after 10 minutes there are still teams in play, they must continue throwing and catching one handed until elimination.
Safety:	No throwing cooler of ice cold Gatorade on winning team.

BEND IT LIKE BECKHAM

Equipment:	Tape to mark off 5 ft. goal space and a soft, small size soccer ball
Area:	15 ft. x 15 ft. approx.
Players:	3 teams of two - One goalie, one penalty kicker, one referee, a throng of adoring fans.
Type:	Team
Time:	15 minutes max
Objective:	Kick the goal past the goalie as many times as possible in 5 minutes
Directions:	Mark off a 5 ft. long and 2 ft. deep goal area. Penalty kicker can place ball anywhere they desire to launch kick. Kicker gets a point for every goal scored. Goalie gets a point for every goal blocked. Kicks not in goal area or outside goal area are not counted.
Safety:	No walloping kicks to the goalie or head butting. This isn't the World Cup.

OFFICE AIRLINES

Equipment:	Printed, non-offensive emails, markers, paperclips
Area:	15 ft. x15 ft.
Players:	2 per team - 4-5 teams
Type:	Team
Time:	10 minutes
Objective:	Fly your team's plane the farthest
Directions:	Each team of two creates a paper airplane they feel will travel a long distance. Each team must name their airline and decorate their plane accordingly with magic markers. Planes are limited to one piece of paper and may use one small paperclip anywhere on the plane if needed. The team with the plane traveling the longest distance wins a small bag of peanuts and 1/4 can of soda.
Safety:	Beware of paper cuts and baggage handler strikes.

OFFICE PICTIONARY

Equipment:	Large white sheets of paper, presentation easel and thick Sharpie markers OR white dry erase board and erasable thick markers. 3x5 cards with your company's commonly used terms, slogans and vocabulary printed on them.
Area:	10 ft. x10 ft.
Players:	2 per team - 4-5 teams 1 timekeeper from a competing team
Type:	Team
Time:	20-30 minutes

Objective: Your partner draws a picture that explains card. You have 30 seconds to guess what they're drawing. Or vice versa.

Directions: Each team of two decides who will draw and who will guess first. The drawing team member chooses a card from the deck with a company phrase or slogan printed on it. The timekeeper gives the go. The person at the board begins drawing what is printed on the card as the other team member begins to guess. They have 30 seconds to guess the drawing. A point is awarded for each correct answer. Teams take turns at the board. When all the teams have taken their first turn at the board another round begins with the drawer and guesser switching positions.

Safety: This game has been known to ruin friendships and incite physical violence. Proceed with care.

ALPHA HUNT

Equipment: Paper grocery bag and marker for each team. List of alphabetical items

Area: Large common space

Players: 2 per team - 4-5 teams

Type: Team

Time: 10 minutes

Objective: Collect an item for every letter of the alphabet in the least amount of time. Each item collected is worth 1 point.

Directions: Two members of an opposing team or designated scorekeepers hide 26 objects A-Z around a common area. The hidden pieces are small and must not be hidden with too much difficulty. The team has a bag with their name on it and a list of alphabetical items. One member of the two person team begins the hunt when the time keeper starts the clock. The team member manning the bag and list of items can coach and yell out items that need to be found from the bag from their position at the bag station and is also permitted to direct the searching team mate toward objects they can spot from their vantage point. At 5 minutes time, team members switch.

1. Every item must fit inside the bag.

2. Each item can only be used for one letter.

3. One point per letter.

4. The team finding the most articles in the least amount of time wins.

Safety: Don't hide objects in places that are too hard to reach or require standing on additional stools or chairs to retrieve.

UNRAVELED

Equipment: Ball of kite string or yarn for each team. Large metal binder clip for each team.

Area: 20 ft. x20 ft. room or hallway

Players: 5 per team - 3-4 teams - assembled in circles facing inward

Type: Team

Time: Shortest time

Objective: Race to unravel and rewind string with binder clip still attached.

Directions: The starting team member holds the ball of string and the binder clip. On 'GO' signal, the team member keeps hold of the end of the string, but hands the ball of string to his neighbor. He then slides the binder clip onto the end of the string and slides it down the string to his neighbor. In this manner, the ball of string is passed around the circle with the binder clip following right behind.

When the string is completely unwound, tie the binder clip to the end of it and wind the ball of string back up as it is passed backwards around the circle. Points can be awarded for speed and size of finished ball - smaller is worth more.

Safety: None. Make it a bloody free for all.

MYSTERY CELEBRITY

Equipment: Small pieces of paper with names of famous people written on them

Area: 20 ft. x 20 ft.

Players: 3 per team - 4-5 teams

Type: Team

Time: 10 minutes

Objective: By asking yes or no questions, solve the riddle of the mystery celebrity.

Directions: One team leader goes to the moderator and receives a small piece of paper with the name of a Hollywood celebrity, or a political figure, historical or sports figure.

Each team leader goes to a team, other than his own where the opposing teams asks Yes-or-No questions to figure out who the team leader is.

The first team to yell out the correct name wins 1 point. After a number of rounds, the team with the most points wins

BLIND FOLD PUTTING

Equipment:	A coffee mug, a putter, a golf ball, blindfold, trashcans, boxes, plants for obstacles
Area:	15 ft. x 15 ft.
Players:	Two players per team - 3-5 teams
Type:	Team
Time:	15-20 minutes
Objective:	Communication is key; one team member guides the other to putt the ball into the cup.
Directions:	Each team has three minutes to putt their ball from the starting line into the cup. The putting team member is blindfolded and the second team member gives directions. The course is not without obstacles, and the team member giving direction cannot touch the putting teammate.
Safety:	No swinging at the ball. No playing through.

HOOP ON A LOOP

Equipment:	Hula hoop or an 8 ft. length of rope tied in a circle for each team
Area:	Large open space or hallway
Players:	5-8 per team
Type:	Team
Time:	TBD
Objective:	Working together for a team win
Directions:	Each team stands in a circle, facing inward. The hula hoop or rope circle is hung on one teammate's arm. Team members then join hands to close the circle. On

'GO', each team moves the hoop around their circle from player to player without letting go of hands.

First team to finish 2 or 3 laps wins the gold. Second and third place get silver and bronze.

Safety: Be appropriate.

GREAT BALLS OF PAPER

Equipment: 100 sheets of paper

Area: Large open area or hallway

Players: 3 players per team. Flip a coin to see which teams go first.

Type: Team

Time: :30 per round

Objective: Be the last team standing to win the gold.

Directions: Wad paper into 100 tight balls. Have a team on each side of a center line - you can mark this with tape if needed. Distribute the paper balls across both sides of the playing area. Have an unbiased timekeeper stand at the center line with his back to the play area so he does not see how the game is going. On 'GO' signal, teams throw all the paper from their side to the other side. When the timekeeper yells, 'STOP!' the round ends and balls on each side are counted.

The timekeeper should give about 30 seconds for each round.

Either have the winning team face the next team or record scores and have two new teams play.

Safety: Unlike Dodgeball, the objective of this game is not to pelt players from the opposing team. However it is only paper so... if you're so inclined, aim low.

PERPETUAL MOTION

Equipment: A dozen tennis balls, an impartial judge to survey the action.

Area: 15 ft. x 15 ft.

Players: 3-4 members per team 3 teams

Type: Team

Time: Teams go as long as they can keep the motion going.

Objective: Keep as many objects as possible in constant motion.

Directions: Group stands in a circle. One ball is put in motion and kept in motion, by throwing, bouncing, rolling. Another ball is added, then another. If a ball stops moving, the round is over. Teams can take the time between rounds to plan how to better execute the game for their next turn. Each team should get 2 -3 rounds.

Safety: Pay attention to your partners and spectators.

BLANKET STATEMENT

Equipment: Small blanket, tarp, or piece of fabric, a stopwatch and12 office items or items specific to your company. Choose items that are different sizes and shapes. Example. A paperclip, a CD spindle, a file folder, a set of computer speakers, a push pin, a box of Kleenex, a duffle bag, a company t shirt, etc.

Area: 15 ft.x 15 ft.

Players: 3-5 teams of 2

Type: Team

Time: 10-15 minutes

Objective: Remember the whereabouts of all the items under the blanket.

Directions: Find a dozen office items from around the area and spread them out on the ground. On a piece of paper, diagram the layout of the items for later scoring.

Cover the items with the blanket gather the teams around it.

Remove the blanket and give them one minute to study the items. Cover the items again.

The teams must remain in silence for one minute after the blanket is replaced. After one minute has passed, the teams have 8 minutes to remember not only all the items under the blanket but where they were placed. The teams are given a blank piece of paper and must make heir own diagram of the layout of the items. If a team completes the diagram before the 8 minutes are up, the team must yell out to the judge and the game stops. All remaining team communication must stop until the diagram is verified as correct. If it is not 100% correct, the game resumes until another team finishes their diagram or the 9 minutes is up.

When the time is up, the team with the most correct objects on their diagram wins the gold.

Each correct answer is worth 2 points

OPTION: You may allow players to re-examine the originals at a cost of 1 point per second per person. So, if two people look for 8 seconds, that costs 16 points.

Safety: No touching the blanket to feel for objects. If you have X-ray vision, good sportsmanship dictates you refrain from using it.

AD EXEC FOR A DAY

Equipment: Dry erase board, chalkboard or large pad of paper

Area:	Medium to large open space
Players:	5-7 max
Type:	Team
Time:	TBD
Objective:	To examine the power of agreement in a collective goal; looking at the ideas of another person as a catalyst for productivity rather than a challenge.
Directions:	Assemble group of five to seven people who will create a full marketing campaign for an imaginary product, including product name, slogan, 30 second commercial, celebrity spokesperson, jingle, and marketing plan, meeting each idea presented with enthusiastic agreement.

Participants are separated into equal teams and assigned an imaginary product such as: Internet bread toaster, pedal-less bicycle, toothless comb, bottomless bottle of wine, vertical bed, a 3 second jumpback time machine, always pay slot machine, etc. Or you can create products or services for your specific industry.

Take the first three minutes for idea generation. All ideas must be used or incorporated. Take the next five minutes to create the elements of the campaign. The final remaining time should be used rehearse their pitch and 30 second commercial for the product that contains all of the required elements (name, jingle, celebrity spokesperson, etc.) within the commercial.

Using only props from the office, each team then performs their 30 second commercial for the judges and other teams. Judges award points for categories such as most creative, best production, best impersonation of a celebrity, etc.

Safety:	No secret video taping of commercials and posting on Youtube.

CHAPTER 11
OFFICE SPORTZ HALL
OF FAME- ELEVATOR

OFFICE GAMES "ELEVATE" ADMINISTRATIVE ASSISTANT TO NEW HEIGHTS

Gloria Jamison didn't think her ability to see into the future would ever come in handy working in the admissions office at Houston Community College in Houston, Texas.

"My job is mostly filing and collating" said the plucky intern-turned-admin assistant. "I know what the next file is but that doesn't make it get filled any faster now does it? No, it does not. I really thought this position was going to be the first in a series of dead end jobs- that is until we held this year's office games!"

Gloria saw her opportunity to shine when she signed on to join the Office Sportz "Who's on the Elevator" team.

"I got 6 out of 10 people who got off the elevator correct and that gave our team the advantage which led us to the gold. I knew I had "the gift"- ya know, every once in a while naming which song would come on the radio next or saying to people around me, "I KNEW you were gonna say that!" right after they said something. But my telepathy only spans a short time before something is going to happen- 2 or 3 minutes tops."

With her new found confidence in predicting the future, Gloria is looking ahead and setting new career goals for herself. She states that she would like to possibly move from administrative duties to a guidance counselor role at the college.

"Who knows? If I really hone my skills I may be able to tell students what careers they're going to end up in after graduation. That way they could take classes that would help them in those professions. I mean, if someone's going to be a banker I'll tell them to ditch those boring English Lit classes 'cuz you don't need to know Chaucer to figure out interest rates. I want to use my gifts for good, you know? Office Sportz has helped me realize my amazing abilities and unlimited potential. Without "Who's on the Elevator" I may have never found my true calling," she concludes. "But since I'm so obviously psychic, I probably would have figured it out ....eventually."

CHAPTER 12
AWARDS CEREMONIES

The award ceremonies serve two critical purposes:

1. The winners get stuff.

2. Signifies the end of the games and the beginning of the party!

In all seriousness, the awards ceremony is a great way to extend the good feelings generated by the games beyond the closing ceremony. Awards can be displayed with pride while reminding everyone of the fun they all had together.

Creating the awards can be as simple as purchasing some plastic medals from the local party store or creating them from a string of paper clips and some yogurt caps. Be inventive. The wackier the award medals the more cherished they become to the winners.

If you really want to be Politically Correct, you could have awards for all of the athletes but there is a growing body of scientific evidence that shows awarding everyone a prize simply for competing dampens the inner fire that often produces great athletes. Okay, we made that last part up but otherwise how are the winners going to rub the loser's nose in it until the next set of games?

CONCLUSION

Hopefully by now you have already enjoyed the surprising amount of fun and teambuilding Office Sportz can bring to an office. However, in order to keep this level of camaraderie going, it is incumbent upon you to stoke the fires occasionally by continuing what you started. Hold events bi-annually or play a quick game right before a long meeting or to break up a long meeting or instead of a long meeting.

Once you have begun creating an engaging environment invite others to create events or share ideas that will serve to bring your group closer together. Most important, don't forget that work is a four letter word so the next time someone asks you what you do for a living, tell them that you are an Office Athlete!

AFTERWORD

Think OfficeSportz is a great idea but would love to have someone else be in charge? We've got you covered! OfficeSportz has teamed up with the premier improvisational comedy performers in the country to bring you OfficeSportz LIVE! Now you can enjoy the games as a participant while a professionally trained improvisational performer acts as Host, Judge, Referee, and all around ringmaster for your OfficeSportz Event

Office Sportz always tailors itself to your group, and it's always positive, hilarious and clean. Some of our corporate clients include:

Allied Van Lines   Abbott Labs
McDonalds   Bayer
Anheuser Busch   City of Las Vegas
Terex   Schneider Electric
Major League Baseball   BP
Pepsi   Ovation Pharmaceuticals
Waste Management   Old Navy
Allied   7UP
Century 21   Home Depot
GM   CNA
Bank of America   Dixie
Motorola   Florsheim
International   Cure Autism Now
Borders Bookstores   Cadillac
Ford   Miller Lite
Merck   StorageTek
IBM   NXTComm
Ford   Daimler Chrysler
Burger King   Chicago Tribune
Coors Light   Staples
Sun Microsystems   New York Film Festivals
DMB&B   Sears

For more information, pricing, and availability visit us on the web at
www.OfficeSportz.com.

Have fun and let the games begin!

ACKNOWLEDGEMENTS

This book would not have been possible without the sincere love and utter patience of my wife Leane and daughter McKenna, both of whom are enduring beacons of light and laughter and without whom my ship would not only be rudderless but very poorly decorated.

Bob and Marge Rogers and the entire extended Rogers clan whose numbers grow exponentially while our bonds grow ever stronger.

If you are looking to truly improve the quality of your life then you can do no better than picking up Vince Poscente's InVinceable Principles, The Ant and the Elephant, and the New York Times Bestseller, The Age of Speed. Vince takes smart, funny, and dynamic to a whole new level. Visit him at www.vinceposcente.com - no, seriously, visit him right now!

After you have read those books you can let everyone know how wonderful you have become by reading the New York Times Bestseller, Life is a Series of Presentations by Mr. Presentation (tm), Tony Jeary. A wonderful strategic facilitator and gifted coach who literally wrote the book on success acceleration. Visit him at www.tonyjeary.com.

Mike Muetzel knows so much about Gen X you'd think he was a member of Pearl Jam. While not exactly a Seattle grunge king, Mike is a super successful salesman, management guru, and author of "They're Not Aloof... Just Generation X." Visit him at www.mxmuetzel.com

Every corporate client of Zap Creative Inc. who has been gracious enough to not only to hire me in my secret identity as a Strategic Corporate Communications Creative Director and Professional Emcee but shared with me the innumerable stories and nightmares that can only occur in office life.

Mark Owen and Tony Lorenz who got me started in this business. Vicky and Duffy Swift, Marty Zitlin, and Sharon Wilson who helped me stay in business, and the countless other production companies who keep giving me the business...I meant that in the nicest possible way.

Last, but not least, my sister Kay, who not only helped me with this book but helped me get started in my career as an actor. I wish I could write half as well as her. Check out her stories of growing up and living in Chicago at http://www.chicagomuses.blogspot.com

To anyone I may have omitted, my sincere apologies and gratitude.

ABOUT THE AUTHORS

Jeff Rogers is President and Chief Creative Officer of Zap Creative, Inc (www.zapcreativeinc.com) a strategic communications company based in Chicago. He is also known by thousands of corporate clients through his work onstage as a professional emcee and host for corporate meetings and events.

A veteran of the famous Second City Theater in Chicago, Jeff performed with comedic stars such as Steve Carell from The Office, Stephen Colbert from The Colbert Report, Saturday Night Live alum and current 30 Rock stars Tina Fey and Rachel Dratch, Nia Vardalos, Ian Gomez, from My Big Fat Greek Wedding and Amy Sedaris.

Jeff is currently working on his second book "The Power of PLAY" which teaches individuals how to create an environment conducive to success through our ability to PLAY.

Kate Porterfield is a clinical psychologist and a facilitator of Improvisational workshops and classes. Trained at the legendary Second City, Kate performed, taught and directed with the Detroit company and went on to launch The Second City Training Center in New York. As a group facilitator, Kate has developed and led workshops and interactive programs for organizations seeking to heighten creativity, strengthen communication and media skills, and enhance team collaboration. Kate's clients have included Major League Baseball, Pfizer Pharmaceuticals, MTV, Staples and the National Hockey League. Kate is on staff at Bellevue Hospital in New York City and a clinical instructor at New York University School of Medicine.

Maria Corell began her entertainment career in Chicago performing with the Second City National Touring Company and writing and directing for Second City Communications. Maria also co-wrote and starred in the nationally syndicated sketch comedy television show, The Sports Bar and later became Producing Artistic Director of the Second City Cleveland. She was also a member of the Zap Creative, Inc. team , writing strategic corporate communications elements for such clients as: IBM, Motorola, GM, Ford, Chrysler, Abbott Labs, Schering Plough, Bayer, Little Caesars' Pizza, BP, Staples, McDonald's, Burger King, Church's fried Chicken, Staples, Schneider Electric, Border's, 7UP, Pepsi, Coors Light, CNA, Bank of America, Century 21, DMB&B, UTY, Sears, American Bottling Company, Allied Van Lines, and Waste Management to name a few.

Made in the USA